Cromosys Publication

English
Voice
Accent and
Pronunciation

NIRANJAN JHA SHOWMAN

Founder - Niranjan Jha Showman

cromosys ®
Corporation
Education and Technology Research Center
Patankar Park, Nallasopara (W), Mumbai. +91-9561450045
Education, Technology, Publication, Healthcare, Newsmedia, Realtor, Filmmaking
www.facebook.com/cromosys

+91-9561450045
Learn Advanced Skills
And Get Job Instantly
GERMAN
Python
FRENCH
C++
SPANISH
Java
ENGLISH
HTML5
RUSSIAN
CSS
JavaScript
Cromosys
Education and Technology Research Center
Nallasopara (W), Mumbai

Learn Web Programming
Demo-Class Free
HTML
CSS
React
JavaScript
Typescript
Bootstrap
Cromosys
20 Years of Experience
Nallasopara (W), Mumbai
+91-9561450045

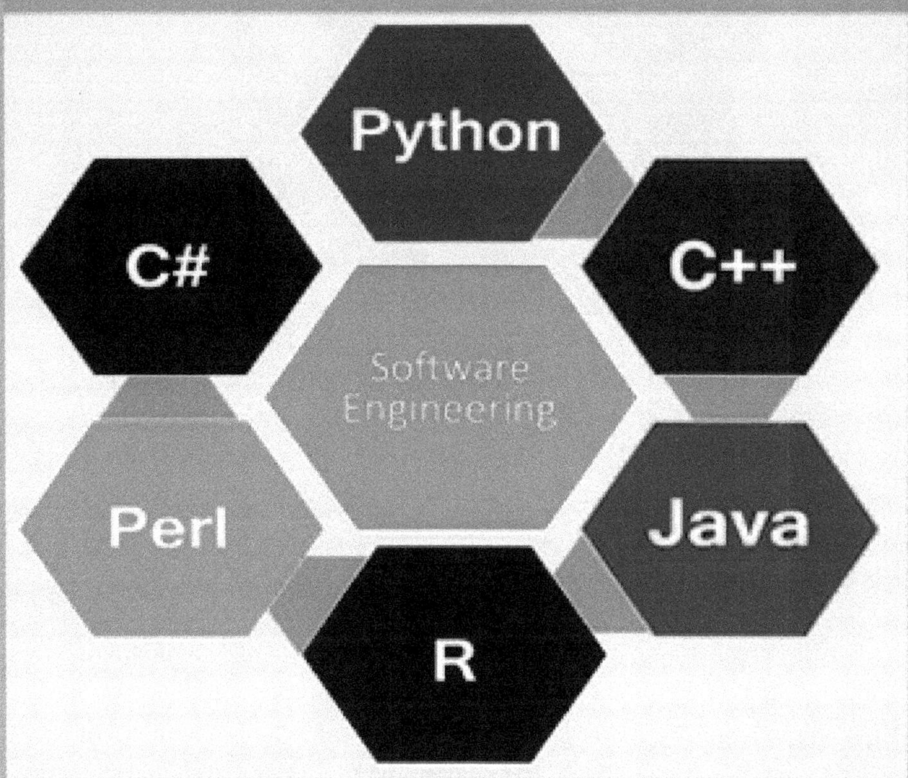

+91-9561450045
Learn Software Engineering
Demo-Class Free
Python
C#
C++
Software
Engineering
Perl
Java
R
Cromosys
20 Years of Experience
Nallasopara (W), Mumbai
+91-9561450045

25 Years of Experience
Learn Visual Multimedia
Animation VFX
Movie Editing
Game Development
Cromosys
+91-9561450045
Education and Technology Research Center
Nallasopara (W), Mumbai
www.facebook.com/cromosys

Jobs Available
For Candidates Who Know

German
French
Spanish

Vacancy in Germany, France, Spain

For Hospitality, Engineering, IT Sector

With Free Visa, Airfare and Accommodation

Cromosys

Education and Technology Research Centre

Nallasopara (W), Mumbai

+91-9561450045

20 Years of Experience

+91-9561450045

Foreign Languages Institute
German, French, Spanish
Basic and Advanced - All Levels
3 x 6 = 18 Courses
FRANCHISE
Business Offer
Teaching Materials Provided
We have 1 Million Students Globally
Great Income Assured
Global Exposure
Cromosys
20 Years of Experience
Nallasopara (W), Mumbai
+91-9561450045

Cromosys Publication

English Voice Accent and Pronunciation

Niranjan Jha Showman

"Education taken with zeal educes to success."
~Niranjan Jha Showman

Preface

Cromosys Publication's "English Voice Accent and Pronunciation" book is an optimal quality guide to the beginners as well as advanced learners who want to gain real knowledge of English Accent, Diction, and Voice Modulation. It is an unmatchable unique book of its kind that guarantees your improvement on your speech. The lessons and study materials uniquely designed are based on my fifteen years of research in linguistic field. The text, audio and video are magnificently powerful to bringing you in the light of phonology. Since English is accepted as a global language, people around the world have been sharpening their knowledge to be good in it. Sometimes, only working knowledge of English doesn't work, and you feel that there is a lot more to explore. The accurate and profound pronunciation of this language, which was considered to be existing only in England and America in past, has influenced zillions of mind today. Therefore I conceived the idea of making this book a guideline for those who want to be perfect in English Pronunciation and speak like native English speakers.

The significance of this book is that it is dynamic, systemic and blissful with abundance of pure and perfect set of rules that took a decade of time in preparation. For learning English pronunciation, one being immaturely suggested, spends ages in reading literature, watching movies and listening to the audio which help them to imitate a little but doesn't make them as perfect as they want to be. The real technique of English pronunciation is something different and that difference is clearly written and explained in this book. A careless learner, with their never-ending process of Picasso Adventure collects some scattered information which is unworthy to phonological approach. And the aspirants get lost in wilderness. The right way to understand British and American pronunciation is that, you need to look at the IPA (International Phonetic Alphabet) written after every word in this book, and pronounce the words. When needed, you can take help from audios available on Google Translate. But IPA is must to understand the sound correctly.

Cromosys, our education and technology research center, saving human efforts from being wasted, is to make you as good as native English speaker. The world growing with density has brought enormous opportunity to linguistic talents irrespective of their geographical boundaries. Since I got a chance to get myself trained on English accent in the USA and began talking to native speakers around the world while managing a team in several call centers, I got to understand linguistic science. Having been teaching English to global exposure from last thirteen years, I have come across numerous rules of pronunciation which are mistakenly ignored by a great majority of non-native speakers. They don't even believe that there is any rule for pronunciation. And the result gets disgraceful when they accuse Standard English to be outlaw because it shocks them as they don't understand anything from British or American mouth even though having a great knowledge of English Grammar. I strongly believe this book is useful for people working for communication-based industry, media houses, entertainment world, and obviously for those who love English. It will stand a milestone for you in the journey of accent learning, and with your sharpened ability, you can make your way of success without any hindrance. After you start the lesson, you don't need to worry about anything but just follow each and everything carefully. Don't procrastinate and never give up. You are going to do the most beautiful thing for yourself, so be bold enough to complete all the lessons. You may have seen some other English Pronunciation books or CDs full of conversations and dialogues which the students purchase by mistake. But they quit the hope of learning when the conversations say what to do – but "not" how to do. It doesn't explain but keep on speaking or talking only. Just memorizing the words will not take you anywhere. So I have designed this book with proper set of lessons to make you start your adventure sitting at home beginning with real basic. All symbolic hints and lessons explained in this book will guide you to pronounce words correctly as native speaker speaks.

Cromosys, our education and technology research center, which is a path-breaking pioneer training institute for Spoken English, Foreign Languages, and Computer Science, is committed to enlightening human mind with educational endeavors, and we are doing the same from last successful fifteen years. We not only hope but believe that your success is in your hand now, and this book will take you miles ahead in your expectation. We always respect the views and comments of readers, so for any communication with regards to assistance, enquiry or collaboration, we are always at your reach as it helps us improve our ability.

This fact may surprise you that almost seventy percent people of the world even today don't know how to speak proper English. And so, even in this 21st century, a large number of people are away from the benefits of communicating with native speakers. Whether you want to travel abroad or plunge deep into your research, your poor accent or bad pronunciation damages your reputation so much that neither a native speaker can understand you nor you can understand them. You may be very good in writing, but that is not enough today. With the growth of several multinational companies, there is a need of talented people to express clearly in the field of communication. The telecommunication industry has greatly inspired several people to have a good English accent so that the conversation takes place effectively. Being good in English accent and diction is a major advantage in getting a good job.

Niranjan Jha Showman
Trainer, Author Physician, Entrepreneur, Filmmaker, Activist
Founder of Cromosys Corporation
facebook.com/cromosys
+91-9561450045
cromosys@yahoo.com
Nallasopara (W), Mumbai, India

My other books: -
English Word Power
Teach Yourself German
Teach Yourself French
Teach Yourself Spanish
Be millionaire like me
Dynamic Grammar of English
Teach Yourself HTML5
Teach Yourself 3ds Max
Teach Yourself Autodesk Maya

Cromosys Corporation
Education and Technology Research Center
Education, Technology, Publication, Healthcare, Realtor, Filmmaking
facebook.com/cromosys
+91-9561450045
cromosys@yahoo.com
Nallasopara (W), Mumbai, India

About the Author

Niranjan Jha Showman
Trainer, Author, Physician, Entrepreneur, Filmmaker, Activist

Niranjan Jha Showman is a Language Scientist and Technical Researcher. He is the Award Winning author of more than fifty educational and fictional books at Amazon. He is one of the great-grandsons of the first President of India Dr. Rajendra Prasad (from adoption). He is a Public Figure, and the globally - renowned Languages Trainer of French, Spanish, and German from past twenty years. Niranjan Jha Showman is an Entrepreneur and also works as a Filmmaker in India. Being the founder and owner of Cromosys Corporation - a company located in Mumbai, India, his company is excelling in the fields of Education, Technology, Publication, Newsmedia, Realtors, Banking, and Cinemascope from past fifteen years.

Niranjan Jha Showman's good-seller educational books and novels are appreciated worldwide. He has more than one million eBook buyers online, and more than one million learners are connected to him globally. Some of his novels is critically acclaimed. He is the trainer of French, Spanish, German, English Voice and Accent, and Advanced Computer Education. He is also a political activist and the founder of Vikaswadi Party in India.

Niranjan Jha Showman is the man who came from rags to riches, he who knows how to turn the table, and he, whom you call the man of Midas-touch, and Renaissance man. He has observed lives from the Pandora of monkeys to the sanctuary of monks, not only down-to-earth but down-to-grave. He is a B. Com. graduate, and B. Ed. from Delhi University, and diploma holder in French, Spanish and German from America. You can watch his songs, movies, educational videos and many more things by typing "Niranjan Jha Showman" in Google.

Niranjan Jha Showman
+91-9561450045
cromosys@yahoo.com
Nallasopara (W), Mumbai, India
www.facebook.com/cromosys
www.notionpress.com/author/814619
www.facebook.com/niranjanshowman
www.facebook.com/vikaswadiparty

Statutory

This book with its content is the registered property of the author Niranjan Jha Showman.
The author and his Cromosys Publication holds all necessary rights of this book.
The copyright certificate of this book is attached at the end of this book.

Lesson 1
The alphabet pronunciation

For each letter and its examples, the pronunciations are given in the bracket. The pronunciation is in International Phonetic Alphabet (IPA), which is explained at the bottom of the page. In brackets, the bold letter should be stressed while pronouncing. Look at the IPA and pronounce the words with the help of Google Translate audio.

a – (ei)
It is a stretched sound. Examples: - d<u>a</u>te – (**d**eit), g<u>a</u>te – (**g**eit), <u>A</u>sia – (**ei**ʃə), bio-d<u>a</u>ta – (baiəu-**d**eitə), mist<u>a</u>ke – (mis**t**eik)

b – (bhi)
It is a soft sound. Examples: - <u>b</u>achelor – (**b**ætʃlə), <u>b</u>oyfriend – (**b**awifrend), a<u>b</u>duct – (æb**d**əkt), <u>b</u>iology – (bai**o**lədʒi), alphabet – (**æ**lfəbet)

c – (ssi)
It is a snake (sibilance) sound. Examples: - <u>c</u>ell – (**s**el), de<u>c</u>ent – (**d**eesnt), suc<u>c</u>ess – (sək**s**es), velo<u>c</u>ity – (və**l**osəti), essen<u>c</u>e – (**e**sns)
The examples of 'c' with **k** sound will come under 'k' letter.

d – (dhi)
It is a soft sound. Examples: - <u>D</u>enmark – (**d**enmaak), i<u>d</u>ea –(ai**d**eeə),<u>d</u>octor – (**d**oktə), deo<u>d</u>orant – (diə**u**dərənt), han<u>d</u>icraft–(**h**ændikraaft)

Hints:-
ei – as in cake, ʃ - as in ship, ə- as in ago (half a), əu- as in go (o+u), æ – as in cat, aw – as in saw, dʒ - mixed sound of d+zh, ai – as in my, tʃ - as in chest

You may not understand a few things of IPA in first lesson, but as you move ahead, things would be getting clear to you. For audio help, listen to the pronunciation of each word by typing it in the search box of <u>www.webster.com</u>, or download a <u>talking dictionary</u> from internet. While practicing, you can record your own voice to make sure you are pronouncing correctly, and write the pronunciation in your notebook as well.

Read this passage with energy, clarity and correct pronunciation.

A man found a cocoon for a butterfly. One day a small opening appeared, he sat and watched the butterfly for several hours as it struggled to force its body through the little hole. Then it seemed to stop making any progress. It appeared as if it had gotten as far as it could and could go no farther. Then the man decided to help the butterfly. He took a pair of scissors and snipped the remaining bit of the cocoon. The butterfly then emerged easily. Something was strange. The butterfly had a swollen body and shriveled wings. The butterfly spent the rest of its life crawling around with a swollen body and deformed wings. It was never able to fly. What the man in his kindness and haste did not understand, was that the restricting cocoon and the struggle required for the butterfly to get through the small opening of the cocoon are God`s way of forcing fluid from the body of the butterfly into its wings so that it would be ready for flight once it achieved its freedom from the cocoon. Sometimes struggles are exactly what we need in our life.

Lesson 2
The alphabet pronunciation

Diction, which means the art of speaking clearly so that each word is clearly heard and understood to its fullest complexity and extremity, and concerns pronunciation and tone, rather than word choice and style. Working upon the improvement of accent is not hard but easy and interesting. It needs your regular practice with patience and positive attitude. Look at the IPA and pronounce the words with the help of Google Translate audio. These lessons have only those alphabets in list which are pronounced differently from the general perception of the non-native English speakers. A good command over pronunciation can be gained only when these letters are pronounced correctly. These lessons require utmost seriousness while practicing. Once you are thorough with one pronunciation only then jump to another.

f – (ef)
It is a close-lips sound. Examples: - father – (**f**aathə), infant – (infənt), after – (**aa**ftə), Microsoft – (**m**aikrəusoft), philosophy – (fəlosəfi)

g – (dʒi)
It is a mixed sound of d+zh. It has a soft sound like 'gh'. Examples: - gallon – (**g**æln), ignite – (ig**n**ait), Uganda – (yu**g**aandə), polygamy – (pəligəmi), intrigue – (in**t**reeg)
The examples of 'g' with **j** sound will come under 'j' letter.

h – (h)
Examples: - hello – (hələu), hero – (**h**irəu), bohemian – (bəu**h**eemiən), havoc – (**h**ævək), Fahrenheit – (**f**ærənhait)

j – (dʒei)
It is a mixed sound of d+zh. Examples: - job – (**dʒ**ob), jester – (**dʒ**estə), eject – (i**dʒ**ekt), hydrogen – (**h**aidrədʒən), gorgeous – (**g**awrdʒəs)

Hints:-
aa – as in mark, o – as in got, ee – as in see, i – as in rich, e – as in let

Oral Reading
Read this passage with energy, clarity and correct pronunciation.

In ancient times, a king had a boulder placed on a roadway. Then he hid himself and watched to see if anyone would remove the huge rock. Some of the king's wealthiest merchants and courtiers came by and simply walked around it. Many loudly blamed the king for not keeping the roads clear, but none did anything about getting the stone out of the way. Then a peasant came along carrying a load of vegetables. Upon approaching the boulder, the peasant laid down his burden and tried to move the stone to the side of the road. After much pushing and straining, he finally succeeded. After the peasant picked up his load of vegetables, he noticed a purse lying in the road where the boulder had been. The purse contained many gold coins and a note from the king indicating that the gold was for the person who removed the boulder from the roadway. The peasant learned what many of us never understand. Every obstacle presents an opportunity to improve our condition.

Lesson 3
The alphabet pronunciation

k – (kei)
It is a soft sound. Examples: - kite – (kait), economics – (ekənomiks), executive – (igzekyətiv), conscience – (konʃəns), schizophrenia – (skitsəfreeniə)

o – (əu)
It is a long sound. Examples: - go – (gəu), depot – (depəu), melodious – (mələudiəs), sociology – (səusiolədʒi), omega – (əumigə)

p – (phi)
It is a soft sound. Examples: - parrot – (pærət), peasant – (peznt), impurity – (impyurəti), apologize – (əpolədʒaiz), development – (diveləpmənt)

r – (aar)
It is a rolling sound. Examples: - rich – (ritʃ), sure – (ʃuər), reservation – (rezəveiʃn), intrusion – (introoʒn), romantic – (rəumæntik)

Hints:-
y – as in yes, ʒ- as in vision, u – as in do, oo – as in too, ʌ– as in cup

Oral Reading
Read this passage with energy, clarity and correct pronunciation.

A lady was giving a speech in a seminar. She was saying that there is a huge difference between growing older and growing up. If you are nineteen years old and lie in bed for one full year and don't do one productive thing, you will turn twenty years old. If I am eighty-seven years old and stay in bed for a year and never do anything I will turn eighty-eight. Anybody can grow older. That doesn't take any talent or ability. The idea is to grow up by always finding the opportunity in change. The elderly usually don't have regrets for what we did, but rather for things we did not do. The only people who fear death are those with regrets. She concluded her speech by courageously singing The Rose. She challenged each of us to study the lyrics and live them out in our daily lives. At the years end Rose finished the college degree she had begun all those years ago. One week after graduation Rose died peacefully in her sleep. Over two thousand college students attended her funeral in tribute to the wonderful woman who taught by example that it's never too late to be all you can possibly be.

Lesson 4
The alphabet pronunciation

s – (ess)
It is a snake (sibilance) sound. Examples: - sailor – (**s**eilər), suspension – (səs**p**enʃn), sovereignty – (**s**ovrənti), devastation – (devəs**t**eiʃn), science – (**s**aiəns)

t – (thi)
It is a soft sound. Examples: - ticket – (**t**ikit), moustache – (məs**t**aaʃ), politician – (polə**t**iʃn), aptitude – (**æ**ptityood), enthusiast – (in**th**yoozi**æ**st)

v – (vhi)
It is a bite-lips sound. Examples: - very – (**v**eri), vampire – (**v**æmpair), vagabond – (**v**ægəbond), provoke – (prə**v**əuk), poverty – (**p**ovəti)

w – (dʌblyoo)
It is a rolled-lips sound. Examples: - water – (**w**awtə), wave – (**w**eiv), Wednesday – (**w**enzdei), underworld – (ʌndə**w**ərld), overweight – (əuvə**w**eit)

z – (zed)
Examples for z: - zealous – (**z**eləs), zero – (**z**irəu), wisdom – (**w**izdəm), zigzag – (**z**igzæg), Amazon – (**æ**məzən)

Oral Reading
Read this passage with energy, clarity and correct pronunciation.

Right after I left the library last night, it started raining. I tried to hail a taxi, but it was useless. They were all filled with last-minute shoppers laden with Valentine's Day gifts for their loved ones. It was really a hassle holding an umbrella in one hand and an armload of hooks in the other. After a while, a nice little old lady rolled down her car window and offered me a ride. Getting in the vehicle, I slipped and fell into a mud puddle, spilling my books all over the road. What a relief it was to finally get home, plop down on the sofa and relax. I slept till six o'clock in the morning, and then, after having breakfast I left for my office.

Lesson 5
Days, Months and Numbers

Monday – (**m**ʌndei)
Tuesday – (**t**yoozdei)
Wednesday – (**w**enzdei)
Thursday – (**th**ərzdei)
Friday – (**f**raidei)
Saturday – (**s**ætərdei)
Sunday – (**s**ʌndei)

January – (**dʒ**ænyuəri)
February – (**f**ebruəri)
March – (**m**aatʃ)
April – (**ei**prəl)
May – (**m**ei)
June – (**dʒ**oon)
July – (dʒulai)
August – (**aw**gəst)
September – (sep**t**embə)
October – (okt**ə**ubə)
November – (nəu**v**embə)
December – (di**s**embə)

One – (wʌn)
Two – (too)
Three – (three)
Four – (fawr)
Five – (faiv)
Six – (siks)
Seven – (seven)
Eight – (eit)
Nine – (nain)
Ten – (ten)
Eleven – (i**l**evn)
Twelve – (**t**welv)
Thirteen – (thər**t**een)
Fourteen – (fawr**t**een)
Fifteen – (fif**t**een)
Sixteen – (siks**t**een)
Seventeen – (seven**t**een)
Eighteen – (ei**t**een)
Nineteen – (nain**t**een)
Twenty – (**t**wenti)

Lesson 6
Diphthonants

Diphthonants are the consonants which is a combination of more than one sound. A proper understanding and practice is required while going through this lesson. Look at the IPA and pronounce the words with the help of Google Translate audio.

ch – (tʃ)
It is a combined sound of t+sh. The diphthonant 'ch' does not have an independent sound in English.
chair – (tʃeə), chain – (tʃein), chicken – (tʃikin),mischievous – (mistʃivəs), research – (risərtʃ)

sio – (ʒ)
It is a combined sound of z+h. It is a unique sound adopted in English from French.
vision – (viʒn), pleasure – (pleʒə),diversion – (daivərʒn), euthanasia – (yoothəneiʒə), déjà vu – (deiʒəvoo), regime – (reʒim)

th– (θ)
This sound is articulated placing the tongue in the middle of upper and lower teeth.
thin – (θin), thirst – (θərst), lethal – (leeθl), menthol – (menθawl), theory – (θiəri)

th–(ð)
This sound is articulated from upper pallet with the touch of tongue.
there – (ðeər), rhythm – (riðəm), southern – (sʌðən), bathe – (beið), without – (wiðawt)

To get the proper pronunciation after reading the IPA, you can take help from Google Translate or Oxford or Cambridge websites. After you gain confidence, you can speak the same word in Google Translate and check whether it types your word. If it types, you win the game! You can also record your own voice to check improvement on your speech.

Oral Reading
Strictly for correct pronunciation

Victor Vickerson was very vivacious and viral virtual man. Betty bought some butter but the butter was bitter so Betty bought some more butter to add to the butter to make the bitter butter better. Daddy drove to Darlington to meet dear Danny who lived in his den. The chair and the box were on the table but the AC was at the airport. Jumping jack was just jumping to jump into the jeep. He drank ooze that was in booze bottle. Do you want to take the pleasure to measure the treasure? A gregarious gaggle of geese started giggling on towards Greece, when a goose with both goggles and candor said to the land in Uganda.

Lesson 7
Polyphones
A letter which has more than one sound is called polyphone.

a

a̲sk– (aa) (**aa**sk)
tha̲t– (æ) (**ð**æt)
a̲go – (ə) (**ə**go)
a̲ll – (aw) (**aw**l)
la̲te – (ei) (**l**eit)
wra̲th – (o) (**r**oð)
pa̲rent – (e) (**p**erənt)
ima̲ge – (i) (**i**midʒ)

e

pe̲n – (e) (**p**en)
wome̲n – (i) (**w**imin)
café̲ – (ei) (**k**æfei)
fe̲male – (ee) (**f**eemeil)
pe̲rson – (ə) (**p**ərsn)

i

di̲g– (i) (**d**ig)
ti̲me – (ai) (**t**aim)
poli̲ce – (ee) (**p**əlees)
shi̲rt – (ə) (**ʃ**ərt)

o

o̲n – (o) (**o**n)
go̲–(əʊ) (**g**əu)
do̲– (u) (**d**u)
sho̲rt(aw) (**ʃ**awrt)
o̲nion– (ʌ) (**ʌ**nyən)
o̲ne – (w) (**w**ʌn)
o̲blige – (ə) (**ə**blaidʒ)

u

tu̲b– (ʌ) (**t**ʌb)
pu̲ll – (u) (**p**ul)
ru̲de – (oo) (**r**ood)
pu̲re– (yu) (**py**uər)∗

ea

beat – (ee) (**b**eet)
great – (ei) (**g**reit)
hear – (eeə) (**hee**eər)
learn – (ə) (**l**ərn)
instead – (e) (**in**sted)

Vowel drill
Speak these words clearly to improve your pronunciation.

OOT	OHT	AWT	AHT	AYT	EET
OOD	OHD	AWD	AHD	AYD	EED
OON	OHN	AWN	AHN	AYN	EEN
OOP	OHP	AWP	AHP	AYP	EEP
OOB	OHB	AWB	AHB	AYB	EEB
OOM	OHM	AWM	AHM	AYM	EEM
OOK	OHK	AWK	AHK	AYK	EEK
OOG	OHG	AWG	AHG	AYG	EEG
OOF	OHF	AWF	AHF	AYF	EEF
OOV	OHV	AWV	AHV	AYV	EEV
OOS	OHS	AWS	AHS	AYS	EES

A word with * sign is meant to have another pronunciation also.
To speak correctly, you should be able to recognize the effectiveness of native speakers. Listen to the newscasters on TV, and while watching movies, try to understand the dialogue.

Lesson 8
Polyphones

c
fa<u>c</u>t– (k) (**f**ækt)
<u>c</u>ession – (s) (**se**ʃn)
politi<u>c</u>ian – (ʃ) (polə**t**iʃn)

s
t<u>s</u>unami – (s) (tsoo**n**aami)
re<u>s</u>ume – (z) (**r**ezyumei)
<u>s</u>ugar – (ʃ) (**ʃ**ugə)
lei<u>s</u>ure– (ʒ) (le**ʒ**ə)

t
<u>t</u>uition –(t) (tyuiʃn)*
iner<u>t</u>ia – (ʃ) (in**ə**rʃə)
ges<u>t</u>ure – (tʃ)(**dʒ**estʃə)
debu<u>t</u> – (..) (**d**ebyoo)

x
e<u>x</u>cuse – (ks) (iks**ky**oos)
lu<u>x</u>ury – (kʃ) (**l**ʌkʃəri)
<u>x</u>erox – (z) (**z**iroks)
e<u>x</u>ecutive – (gz) (ig**z**ekyətiv)

y
l<u>y</u>ric – (i) (**l**irik)
x<u>y</u>lophone – (ai) (**z**ailəfəun)
mart<u>y</u>r– (ə) (**m**aartə)
<u>y</u>acht – (y) (**y**ot)*

z
<u>z</u>odiac – (z) (**z**əudiæk)
pi<u>zz</u>a – (ts) (**p**eetsə)

ch
vou<u>ch</u>er – (tʃ) (**v**əutʃə)
eunu<u>ch</u> – (k) (**y**oonək)
<u>Ch</u>ampaign - (ʃ) (ʃæm**p**ein)

If you think you are safe from thievery, think again. Most thefts occur within three miles of the victim's home. People often venture into the streets without giving their valuables a second thought. They leave things out in the open, where thieves can easily spot them. Items worth thousands of dollars can be stolen in a tenth of second. So be thoughtful. Only you can thwart this terrible crime. Watch your things carefully. Thieves do.

Lesson 9
Arabic-Persian Sound

There are some Arabic-Persian words which are widely used in Asia and Middle East. Sometimes, they are used while speaking English also.

q
It gives a heavy aspirated guttural sound.
Quran
Quraish
Iraq
Siddiqui
Qatar

kh
It also gives a heavy aspirated guttural sound.
Khan
Kazakhstan
Khartoum Sudan
Akhtar
Mukhtalif

gh
It is also pronounced with guttural sound.
Afghanistan
Baghdad
Alibagh
Ghalib
Ghaza

The letters z and f of Arabic-Persian language are pronounced same as in English.

Oral Reading
For fast reading and correct pronunciation

On dark nights, I sometimes dream of little dwarfs who like to ride through the woods and along country roads on tiny donkeys. On cold stabbing nights they try to invert riddles to the sound of the winds. They tend to find clear skies disappointing and much prefer dark stormy nights. One such dark stormy dismal night in winter, I observed a dozen of these little men hunting for dandelions in the woods. It was raining hard but in the distance I could see a little figure riding away from me. I followed close behind until the dwarf reached a door through which he disappeared. I knocked hard on the door hoping to catch the glimpse of the little creature and where he lived. All of a sudden I hear a dreadful drumming sound behind me. A little drunken dwarf dressed in a diamond-encrusted cloak was riding past me on a dappled donkey. I tried to address him but with his downcast eyes he trundled down the road into the distance. As the day dawned, I woke from my dream.

Lesson 10
Commonly mispronounced words
Most of the people are unaware of it that when a word changes its form, its pronunciation also changes. This lesson is the most valuable for me and I am sure it will be enlightening to you as well.

photograph (**f**əutəgraaf)
photography (fə**t**ogrəufi)
alternate (**aw**ltəneit)∗
alternative (awl**t**ərnətiv)

contribute (kən**t**ribyoot)∗
contribution(kontri**by**ooʃn)
admire (əd**mai**ər)
admirable (**æ**dmərəbl)

capable (**k**eipəbl)
capability (keipə**bil**əti)
able (**ei**bl)
ability (ə**bil**əti)

technique (tek**n**eek)
technician (tek**ni**ʃn)
valid (**v**ælid)
validity (və**lid**əti)

benefit (**b**enifit)
benevolent(bə**n**evələnt)
family(**fæ**məli)
familiar (fə**mi**liər)

configure(kən**fi**gər)
configuration (kənfigə**rei**ʃn)
converse (kən**v**ərs)
conversation(konvə**sei**ʃn)

Oral Reading
I've learned that no matter what happens, or how bad it seems today, life does go on, and it may be better tomorrow. I've learned that you can tell a lot about a person by the way he or she handles a rainy day and lost luggage. I've learned that regardless of your relationship with your parents, you'll miss them when they're gone from your life. I've learned that life sometimes gives you a second chance. I've learned that you shouldn't go through life with a catcher's mitt on both hands. You need to be able to throw something back. I've learned that whenever I decide something with an open heart, I usually make the right decision. I've learned that even when I have pains, I don't have to be one. I've learned that every day you should reach out and touch someone. People love that human touch - holding hands, a warm hug, or just a friendly pat on the back. I've learned that I still have a lot to learn.

Lesson 11
Commonly mispronounced words

component (kəm**p**əunənt)
calamity (kə**l**æməti)
percentage (pə**s**entidʒ)
information(infə**m**eiʃn)
requirement (ri**k**waiəmənt)
obstacle(**o**bstəkl)
colleague (**k**oleeg)
violate (**v**aiəleit)
representative (repri**z**entətiv)
probably (**p**robəbli)
vengeance (**v**endʒəns)
applicable (**æ**plikəbl)
laboratory(lə**bo**rətri)
particular (pə**t**ikyələ)
opportunity (opə**ty**oonəti)∗
available(ə**v**eiləbl)
secretary (**s**ekrəteri)∗
Russia (r∧ʃaa)
rapport (ræ**p**awr)
synthesis (**s**inθəsis
immortality (imawr**t**æləti)
immediately (i**m**eediətli)
vague (**v**eig)
envelope (envələup)
bosom (**b**oozom)

Oral Reading

His dark trench coat immediately caught my attention; I couldn't help but notice his terrific sense of dress. It wasn't anything specific; perhaps it was his attitude that made him stand out. I worked in a government organization. The work was quiet boring. I dealt primarily with purchase details and mortgage payments, and there was just no satisfaction in it. I mean spending the whole day dealing with financial statements, confirming dates and so on – it was absolutely maddening. In the midst of all this, the man in the trench coat remained my focus. I've always met a variety of people but no one matched him in terms of his persona. I suddenly began to realize that I was staring. I had seen an entire transaction occur, the trench coat man passed on a briefcase with an address printed on it. My mind began to churn! What were these men doing? I was soon considering many possibilities as to what these men were up to. They were engaged in a deep conversation. I felt a need to resolve the problem as soon as possible. Finally I thought of a cunning solution. I was going to make a heroine out of myself and placate the situation. I began to make a detailed plan of action where various solutions came to my mind. Firstly, I was going to ask whether their account needed any update. Secondly, if there was any assistance that they needed. I was just about to do this when my mobile phone rang and I saw a vehicle with a running motor standing directly outside the door and suddenly I saw them heading towards the vehicle.

Lesson 12
Minimal Pair
Speak these words loudly to clear out your voice.

Boat   -   Bought
Mad   -   Mud
Hurt   -   Heart
Men   -   Main
Than   -   Then
Bit   -   Bet
Live   -   Leave

I eat it.
The beat was a bit strong.
Give me a kiss for keys.
The chick's cheek is soft.
He did his deed.
These shoes fit my feet.
Martin's grin was green.
Put your heel on the hill.
Let's creep near the crib.
He bumped his lip when he leaped.
He can knit neatly.
We seek the sixth sick sheep.
These are sheep on the ship.
He still steals.
These are better than this one.
Who weeps from the whip?

A fashionably tan man sat casually at the bat stand, lashing a handful of practice bats. The manager, a crabby old bag of bones, passed by and laughed, "You are about average Jack. Can't you lash faster than that?" Jack had had enough, so he clambered to his feet and lashed bats faster than any man had ever lashed bats. As a matter of fact, he lashed bats so fast that he seemed to dance. The manager was aghast. "Jack, you're a master bat lasher!" he gasped. Satisfied at last, Jack sat back and never lashed another bat.

The throng of thermometers arrived on Thursday. There were a thousand thirty three thick thermometers, though, instead of a thousand thirty six thin thermometers, which was three thermometers fewer than the thousand thirty six we were expecting not to mention that they were thick ones rather than thin ones. We thoroughly thought that we had ordered a thousand thirty six, not a thousand thirty three, and asked the folks to reship the thin not thick. They apologized and promised to replace them.

Lesson 13
Etymology
Etymology is the origin and history of a word. After so many years of research, I have brought something which would be very interesting to you.

English
After 500 years of the birth of Jesus Christ, some tribal people living in ANGUL district of Germany moved out of the country and occupied anew land. As they had come from Angul, they were named ANGLE. That is why we have Angle+land= England, and Angle+ish = English.

Japan
This word is originated from Chinese words JIH PUN.
Jih = sun, pun = origin.

Cockroach
In Spanish, cock means bird and roach means fish. This word came into existence because a cockroach can both fly and swim.

Australia
This word came into existence from Latin word australis.
In Latin, australis means southern.

Monalisa
The picture of Monalisa is a mixed appearance of Egyptian god and goddess of love AMON and LISA. The painting was drawn and popularized by Leonardo Da Vinci because of his ambiguous carnal instinct.

Jesus
There is a possibility that this word was coined in French with the help of two French words.
Je = I
Sus = save

Quran
In Arabic, QURRA means read and AAN means this.

Madam
This word is from French. Ma = my, Dame = lady.

Knife
The reason why K comes as a silent letter in this word is that 'knife' came from French word 'CANIF'. When English were making their language, they used NIF as NIFE with symbolic letter K to justify its origin. Most of the words with silent letters have the same kind of history.

Rickshaw
It is a Japanese word JINRIKISHA. jin = person, riki = power, sha = vehicle.

Curfew
It came from French word COUVRIRFEW, which is couvrir = to cover, feu=fire. In old age, the soldiers ordered the people to cover the fine in night.

Lesson 14
Etymology

Answer
This word came from French which is a combination of two words UN and SWEAR.
un = one, swear = swear. In olden time, your reply was valued to be a swearing.

Excuse
The etymology of this word is very interesting. It is combination of two words - EX and ACCUSE.

Alcohol
This word came into existence with the help of Arabic language. In Arabic, al = the, kohl = black powder used in eyes. While making a paste of the black powder, Arabs used to put spirit in it. The same spirit was named ALCOHOL which people started drinking.

Colonel
This word itself is a big mistake in English. This word 'Colonel' is pronounced (karnal) in English.
In French, it is written as 'CORNEL' and pronounced also 'karnal'.
In German, it is written as 'COLONEL' and pronounced also 'kolonel'.
When this word was brought in English, it took the spelling of German and pronunciation of French.

Pizza
It is an Italian word. In Italian, Pizza means PEA, because in pizza peas are used, so it was named.

Eunuch
In Greek, Eunuch means BEDROOM ATTENDANT.
In olden time, the 'Eunuchs' used to be bedroom attendants and guards to the queens.

Wife
In Old English, this word was used as wifman.
Wifman means wife of man.

Mumbai
This word is a combination of two words. MUMBA means a goddess, and AI means mother.

Cot
This word came from KHAT of Hindi language.

Went
In old English, the word WENT was not past form of the verb 'go'. It was the past form of WEND which means: to move or to go. As the usage of WEND decreased in English, so the past form of WEND was taken for the verb GO.

Police
According to Latin language, police word is originated from policy.
So, police means Policy Maintainer.

Lesson 15
Syllable stress

Syllable is a smallest part of a word that cannot be phonetically broken. It has one consonant sound and one or more than one vowel sound. Syllable stress is the raise of your voice at a particular point in a word.

Rule 1
If a word is both a noun and verb, while speaking, if you use it as a noun, you have to emphasize on its first syllable. And, if you use it as a verb, you have to emphasize on its second syllable.

Address (noun)
Add**r**ess (verb)
I gave him my **a**ddress.
I add**r**essed the meeting.

Respect (noun)
Res**p**ect (verb)
He has no **r**espect for her.
You should res**p**ect your elders.

Surprise (noun)
Sur**p**rise (verb)
It is a matter of **s**urprise.
You sur**p**rised him a lot.

The product is in great **d**emand.
She is de**m**anding an explanation.
She is a Muslim **c**onvert.
She chose to con**v**ert.
How can you ob**j**ect this **o**bject?
I'd like to pre**s**ent you with this **p**resent.
The political **r**ebels wanted to re**b**el against the world.
If you per**f**ect your intonation, your accent will be **p**erfect.
She wouldn't per**m**it them to get a **p**ermit.

Rule 2
Compound words take stress on first word.
For examples: - **card** holder, **eye** sight

Rule 3
Short forms take stress on last letter.
For examples: - CN**N**, BB**C**

Lesson 16
Inflection

Inflection is a change in your tone while speaking. You need to stress on a word to convey the right message. A person's accent consists of three parts: pronunciation, intonation, and word stress. Learn to put emphasis and emotion into you speech, and you will see that the meaning will change automatically. You are suggested to learn, practice and sense the beauty of language.

Example 1
"You are fifteen."
"You are fifteen?"

Example 2
I love you.
I **love** you.
I love **you**.

Example 3
My elder sister lives in New York.
It means only my sister, not anyone else's.

My **elder** sister lives in New York.
It means my elder sister, not younger.

My elder **sister** lives in New York.
It means only my sister, not brother.

My elder sister **lives** in New York.
It means she stays there, not just gone as a tourist.

My elder sister lives **in** New York.
It means she is in the city, not outside of it.

My elder sister lives in **New York**.
It means she is in New York, not London.

Example 4
She teaches English in school.
She **teaches** English in school.
She teaches **English** in school.
She teaches English **in** school.
She teaches English in **school**.

Well begun is half done. Now just other half is remaining. Watching English movies can help you a lot improving you accent.

Lesson 17

Emphasis control

Some words changing their forms change their stress point also. In this lesson, you will see the list of words with all of their group words.

image (**i**midʒ), imagine (i**mæ**dʒin), imagined (i**mæ**dʒint), imaginable (i**mæ**dʒinəbl), imaginary (i**mæ**dʒinəri), imaginative (i**mæ**dʒinətiv), imagination (imædʒi**nei**ʃn)

provoke (prə**vəu**k), provoked (prə**vəu**kt), provocative (prə**vo**kətiv), provocation (provə**kei**ʃn), provocationist (provə**kei**ʃnist)

valid (**væ**lid), validate (**væ**lideit), validated (**væ**lideited), validity (və**li**dəti), validation (væli**dei**ʃn), invalid (in**væ**lid), invalidity (invə**li**dəti)

know (**nəu**), knowing (**nəu**ing), known (**nəu**n), (knowledge (**no**lidʒ), knowledgeable (**no**lidʒəbl), acknowledge (ək**no**lidʒ), acknowledgement (ək**no**lidʒmənt)

electric (i**le**ktrik), electrical (i**le**ktrikl), electricity (ilek**tri**səti), electronic (ilek**tro**nik), electrocute (i**le**ktrəkyoot), electron (i**le**ktron)

matter (**mæ**tər), material (mə**ti**riəl), materialize (mə**ti**riəlaiz), materialism (mə**ti**riəlizəm), materialistic (mətiriə**li**stik)

Oral reading
Read as good as you can

James Bond was not having a very good day. He was having an internal conflict about the prime suspect for a dastardly crime that had been committed the previous Friday. The crime involved the theft of an envelope, which contained a secret formula H7 0157, from the office of his boss. Mr. Bond had good reason to suspect a woman, a former sweetheart of his, but his personal relationship with her was starting to conflict with his investigation of the crime. She was the only one who had a permit for that part of the building, and she had had the perfect opportunity to steal the formula. Giving himself plenty of time to perfect his gallant smile, he arrived at her house to subject her to his charm in order to get some information. When James saw her, he instantly felt the spark of his old love, and he longed to envelop her in his arms, but he could not influence her with his charm. In the end she told him that she could not permit him to use their previous acquaintance in order to get information.

Lesson 18
Difficult word pronunciation

vowel (**v**əuəl)
anarchy (**æ**nərki)
telepathy (təlepəθi)
posthumous (**p**ostyuməs)
cuisine (kwi**z**een)
rendezvous (**r**ondivoo)
equilibrium (eekwi**l**ibriəm)
curriculum vitae (kərikyələm **v**eetai)
suggestion (sə**dʒ**estʃən)
deterioration (ditiriə**r**eiʃn)
hierarchy (**h**aiəraarki)
parentheses (pərenθəsis)
mischievous (**m**istʃivəs)
parliament (**p**aarləmənt)
realtor (**r**eeətər)
tentatively (**t**entətivli)
verbiage (**v**erbi-idʒ)
voluptuous (vəlʌptʃuəs)
colloquialism (kələukwiəlizəm)
our (**aar**)
brochure (**b**roʃer)

Oral reading
Read as good as you can

"As you know there is bewildering assortment of values thrust upon each of us for example by family, religion, friends, ads, media, movies, music and many people and groups take their beliefs and values very seriously. They are certain they are right. If you reject their beliefs, you may encounter serious real threats, for example – "You'll burn in hell" or "Get out of my house" or "You will never be happy" or "That will end our relationship." This is playing hard ball. Sometimes, especially when the other person's values and purposes have not been clearly revealed to you early in the relationship, their moral judgment rejection and threats can be very powerful. I will not deceive you about my beliefs nor will I attack your beliefs. I want you to know that I have doubts about the existence of a God but there are certain values I believe in especially the Golden Rule or caring for others. Strange is our situation here upon earth. Each of us comes for a short visit not knowing why yet sometimes seeming to a divine purpose."
Albert Einstein

Lesson 19

Intonation

Intonation is the rise and fall of your voice in speaking when you are using pitch, tone and volume to affect the meaning of what you are saying. The words in bold letters should be emphasized while speaking.

Sing Song Intonation

You try to speak this sentence in such a way as if you are singing a song.
- I don't know why she doesn't love me.
- Do you think he'll come here today?

Jump Up and Step Down

You can stylize your speaking by putting stress on one bold letter word in the beginning and let the remaining part of the sentence go normal.
- I **love** her because she is very beautiful.
- The **dogs** were barking in the dark street.

Peaks and valleys

This intonation shows anger. In this, every alternate word is stressed.
- **Why** can't **you** answer **this** question?
- **May** I **know** why **did** you **call** me **yesterday**?

Choice Question

- Would you like to read **this book** or **that**?
- He is coming on **Monday** or **Tuesday**.

Statement Intonation

- **Dogs** eat **bones** but cats eat **fish**.
- My dog eats **chicken** and **rice**.

Question Intonation

- Tell me **something** about yourself.
- Are you **coming** today?

Number Intonation

- **800434** 4954
- **98 202** 495 45

Adverb and Adjective Intonation

- I'm **very** happy to meet you.
- She is very **honest** with me.

Negative Sentence Intonation

- He is **not** the one you are looking for.
- This will **not** be done until midnight.

Lesson 20
Modulation
Modulation is the changing of the quality of your voice in order to create a particular effect by making it softer and louder.

Voice Projection
A proper breath, while speaking, makes your voice strong and stable. The quality of your voice is projected by the air in your breath. Make your voice soft and strong by proper breathing. Listen to the voice of good speakers and get the ideas of adding qualities to your own voice. Through constant practices in breath support and vocal variety, you will become more at ease in voice and speech performance. You will also become more skilled in critical listening and analysis of other's voices.

MTI Reduction
Mother Tongue Influence is the hardest thing to get rid of. Every language has a particular way of speaking. While speaking, don't down-track English to your native language style. It will harm your tone and the people would not understand what you speak. Never let your sound reveal your regional identity. Remember that you are learning English to communicate with the world and any kind of regional influence will be a hurdle in your path of success.

Pattern Reduction
Murmuring, muttering, yelping and nasality are the bad voice quality. People, who don't care for their voice, get into this bad habit since childhood. If you find your voice being dominated by any of these things, just get out of it as soon as possible.

Broken Statement Reduction
Some people have the habit of speaking half of what they intend to and they leave other half on the listener to understand. This habit damages the effectiveness of speaking. When you start, complete the sentence of your speaking.

Articulation
Articulation is a way of speaking or pronouncing clearly. Try to resonate over your voice so that it can be deep and clear when you speak. Using effective pausing techniques, pitch varieties and volume emphasis are the steps of articulation.

Apply Emotion
You are doing the work because you are willing and you are doing the work because you have to, are the two different things. When you speak, you want that the people should listen to you. People listen to the voice which is interesting to them. Don't speak like a robot with monotonous voice. We human being should speak applying our emotions. The emotions of pleasure, sorrow, hatred, love and liking can be added to the voice while speaking. It makes human sound beautiful and lively.

Lesson 21

Liaison

Liaison is a connection of words that is mostly used by in American English. When a word ends with a consonant sound and the next word starts with a vowel sound – they are connected. The letters a, e, i, o, u are main vowels and w and y are semi-vowels.

Rule 1
S+A = Z
Example: Two year**sa**go.
Pronunciation: (too yeeərzgəu)

Rule 2
T+Y = CH
Example: Se**t y**our watch.
Pronunciation: (setʃawrwawtʃ)

Example: Can I ge**ty**our name?
Pronunciation: (kænaigetʃawrnaim)

Rule 3
D+Y = J
Example: Where di**dy**ou get it?
Pronunciation: (weərdidʒugetit)

Rule 4
S+Y = SH
Example: Did you lea**se y**our car?
Pronunciation: (didʒuleeʃirkaar)

Example: He will noti**ce i**t.
Pronunciation: (heewilnodiʃit)

Rule 5
Z+Y = ZH
Example: Wa**sy**our test hard?
Pronunciation: (waaʒr testhaard)

Oral Speaking
Two months ago. Set your alarm. How did you find it? Did you lease your house? How was your journey? Five days ago. When did you get it? Set your system clock. How was your experience?

The hurly Burly Mirror store at Vermont and Beverly featured hundreds of first-rate mirrors. There were several mirrors on the chest of drawers, and the largest one was turned towards the door in order to make the room look bigger. One of the girls who worked there was concerned that a bird might get hurt by hurtling into its own reflection. She learned by trial and error how to preserve both, the mirror and the birds. Her earnings were proportionately increased at the mirror store to reflect her contribution to the greater good.

Lesson 22

Nativity

There is one more reason why Native Speakers' English you don't understand. The usage or Nativity makes their English sound different and difficult to understand. The purpose of this lesson is to make you familiar with this. It is not necessary that you should use it in your speech, but you should know it to understand them clearly.

Disappearing vowel

Can – is just pronounced like (kn) while using it in a sentence.
I <u>can</u> speak. (kn)
My – is pronounced like (mə).
Here is <u>my</u> book. (mə)
For – is pronounced like (fə)
It's <u>for</u> you. (fə)
Of – is just (əv).
The alarm <u>of</u> morning is ringing. (əv)
Are – is just (ər)
<u>What are</u> you doing here? (wotər)

Contraction

The contractions being used in speech convey different meanings.
He'll do it. = (will do)
He will do it. = (will certainly do)

She can't stay. = (can not)
She can not stay. = (definitely not)

They won't go there. = (will not go)
They will not go there. = (will certainly not go)

Elements of Grammar

The grammar of a language consists of all these nine elements.

Tense
Parts of Speech
Syntax
Punctuation
Narration
Phonology
Etymology
Semantics
Figure of Speech

Lesson 23

American Heritage

This lesson explains particularly those things which are used in American English. The sound variation with letters t, r and glottal stop are used only by Americans. You should understand this so that you can be familiar with these sounds.

Rule 1

T sound

If the letter t comes in the beginning of a word, it is pronounced hard.

Examples: - table, tomorrow, Tarzan, Trinidad.

If the letter t comes in the middle a word, it is pronounced soft.

Examples: - water, meeting, Italian, attack, daughter.

If the letter t comes at the end a word, it is held like silent.

Examples: - put, light, brought, what, might, slot.

Sometimes, the letter d coming at the end of a word is also pronounced like't'.

Examples: - talked (tawkd), versed (vərst), mortgaged (morgadʒt)

Rule 2

NT sound

T and N are so close in mouth that T sounds disappear in American English.

Examples: - interview (inerview), international (inernational), advantage (advenage), interface (inerface), twenty (tweny), printer (priner)

Rule 3

R sound

If the letter r comes in the beginning or middle of a word, it is rolled.

Examples: - rather, mercy, horse, first, paramount, several.

If the letter r comes at the end of a word, it is silent.

Examples: - power, flower, hour, greater, bigger.

Rule 4

Glottal stop

Glottal stop is a strange thing in American English. In some words, if the letter t comes in the middle, it goes completely mute.

Examples: - football (fu..ball), written (wri..n)

Rule 5

American trolley

The **aw** sound becomes **aa** = so doctor is pronounced (daaktə).

The **au** sound becomes **æu** = so house is pronounced (hæus).

The **yu** sound is mostly pronounced **oo** = so new is pronounced (noo).

The **i** sound is mostly pronounced **ai** = so genuine is pronounced (dʒenuain).

The **aa** sound becomes **aw** = so car is pronounced (kawr).

Lesson 24

Pronunciation symbols

You can find out the correct pronunciation of each word in a dictionary with the help of International Phonetic Alphabet. Why it is necessary to learn is that English has only 26 letters but it has 45 sounds in it. To understand these sounds, the knowledge of IPA is necessary. Look at the IPA and pronounce the words with the help of Google Translate audio.

Vowels

æ	cat
e	bed
a:	arm
3:	her
i	sit
i:	see
o	hot
o:	saw
ʌ	run
u	put
u:	too
ə	ago
ai	my
au	how
ei	day
əu	no
eə	hair
iə	near
oi	boy
uə	poor

Consonants

ʃ	she
ʒ	decision
θ	thin
ð	this
ŋ	ring
dʒ	job
tʃ	chip

Oral reading

A dancing contest is going on. They will contest against each other. It is a written contract between two persons. The rubber contracts when heated. Adam is a convict in this case. She will be convicted for the murder. There is a big discount on these items. I will discount if you pay by cash. He gave me an excuse. Please excuse me. He heard the insult. You kept on insulting her. It is a mysterious object. Bob will object to this. Kenya is perfect. I want to perfect this art. He is a rebel. The students rebelled against the new law. William is the suspect. I suspect Martin.

Lesson 25
Some words
Try to pronounce these words correctly.

Massachusetts
Rhode Island
New Hampshire
Pennsylvania
Georgia
Ohio
Kentucky
Michigan
Idaho
San Jose
Utah

Christopher
Nicholas
Jonathan
Benjamin
Samuel
Cameron
Christian
Gabriel
Veronica
Ashley
Samantha
Suzanne
Chelsea

Oral reading

Owning a calendar is always an asset in the academic industry, owning a receipt book even more so. They spent millions to set up the communication industry in just last year. They ordered pizza to lighten the atmosphere, hoping it would be success. The measure of being comfortable lies in how comfortable you are when no one is looking. Being savvy in many arenas is entirely dependent on flexibility and comfort of training facilities. Cabins were constructed by competent engineers from the last decade. Engineers who initiate ideas are usually unable to deliver. He lived in a hotel far away from the crowds and distributed brochures as a career thinking to be an asset. Don't apologies about the development of the balloon industry, it's a competitive market out there. It is a pleasurable treasure to measure the extent of your revision of sounds that are casually placed within each other's vision.

Lesson 26
Listening skill

Listening is a combination of what we hear, what we understand and what we remember. The most basic need of all human needs is the need to understand and be understood. Listening is a two way process. You need to be heard and also need to hear the other person's idea. Being a good listener is equally important as being a good talker. It means paying attention to the context as well as the content. Good listening is a skill and it has to be developed. Most of the native speakers speak at about 160 words per minute. If you read the entire passage below in sixty seconds, you are reading 160 words-per-minute, which the preferred speed.

As a representative of your organization, it is important that you speak clearly. That means you must articulate. It also means that you must speak so that you can be understood. Although, there is no set rate of speech, most expert speakers talk at between one-hundred-forty and one-hundred-sixty words per minute. That is a good speed for verbal communication. It is not too fast to be understood. It does not give the listener the impression that you are under pressure nor is it too slow. The one-hundred-sixty word rate adds an element of dignity to your voice. This rate of speech also gives a sound image to your audience that establishes both you and your company as efficient and well-organized. To give the audience the kind of impression of yourself and your company that you wish, speak correctly. Speak at one-hundred-sixty – that's one-hundred-sixty words per minute.

Techniques

Use Verbal Nods
Verbal nods assure customers that you are listening. For examples: - right, okay, sure, certainly, fine, brilliant, excellent, absolutely, I agree, yes, I see, really.

Clarify
When you are not sure what customers have said, ask questions to help explain their meaning. Probing questions show that you are listening carefully.
"When you say your computer is not working, is it not switching on at all, or it freezes after starting?"

Paraphrase
Develop the habit of restating the customer's message. Then ask the customer if your understanding is correct.
"So what you're saying is that you were supposed to receive a hard drive on Tuesday, is that correct?"

Engage the customer
Encourage customers to participate in the discussion. Ask for clarification. Check for understanding. Ask for feedback.
"Does that make sense?" "How is that going?" "Have you done this before?"

For practice, you can buy IELTS course audio CD which is available worldwide.

Lesson 27
Tone and Expression
Read out the sentences of this lesson following the proper rule of punctuation. As you are developing the art of speaking in you, so when you speak, feel the sense of it.

Punctuation Mark Exercise

Spain is a beautiful country. The beaches are warm, sandy and spotlessly clean.
Spain is a beautiful country; the beaches are warm, sandy and spotlessly clean.
If Spain is a beautiful country, are the beaches warm, sandy and spotlessly clean?
Spain is beautiful! The beaches are warm, sandy and spotlessly clean!
Spain, a beautiful country, has warm, sandy and spotlessly clean beaches.
"Spain is a beautiful country. The beaches are warm, sandy and spotlessly clean," said the teacher.
"Spain," the teacher said, "Is a beautiful country. The beaches are warm, sandy and spotlessly clean."
Spain is a beautiful country; the beaches are warm, sandy and spotlessly clean. Aren't they?
It is not that Spain is not a beautiful country and the beaches are not warm, sandy and spotlessly clean.
Spain ... a beautiful country...the beaches are warm, sandy and spotlessly clean.

Emotion Tone Exercise
While speaking these sentences apply your emotions and pretend as if you are talking to someone.

She loves you because you speak English very well. (Statement)
She loves you because you speak English very well? (Interrogation)
She loves you because you speak English very well. Don't you? (Tag Expression)
She loves you because you speak English very well. (Softness)
She loves you not because you don't speak English very well. (Arrogance)
She would love you if you would speak English very well. (Sadistic)
Who loves you if you speak English very well? (Sarcastic)

Reading with Thought Process Nodding Adjustment
While reading his passage, apply nodding with facial expression taking a minor pause after every stroke.

Deep down here / by the dark water / there lived old Gollum, / a small slimy creature. / I don't know / where he came from, / nor who / or what he was. / He was a Gollum / as dark as darkness, / except for two big round pale eyes / in his thin face. / He had a little boat, / and he rowed about / quit quietly on the lake; / for lake / it was, wide and deep / and deadly cold. / He paddled it / with large feet / dangling over the side, / but never a ripple / did he make. / No he. / He was looking out / of his pale lamp-like eyes / for blindfish, / which he grabbed with his ling fingers / as quick as thinking. / He liked meat too. / He thought well / when he could get it; / but he took care / they never found him out. / He just throttled them behind, / if ever they came down alone / anywhere near the edge of the water, / while he was prowling about. / They seldom did, / for they had a feeling that / something unpleasant was lurking down there, / down at the very roots of the mountain./

Lesson 28
American English

Everyone, who speaks English, has an accent. In the US, there are many different accents among native speakers. An American, born and educated in Chicago may have an accent for a listener who is also American, but from Boston. In the US, the widespread availability of television has led to an accent that is understood nationwide. Local TV newscasters in Seattle have an accent that is the same as the newscasters in Richmond or Virginia. The TV accent is General American Accent also known as General American or CNN English.

American English is based on speech patterns common in the Midwest of the United Sates and those used by many American network television broadcasters. American English was never the accent of the entire nation. Rather, it was derived from a generalized Midwestern accent and is spoken particularly by many newscasters, in the part because the national broadcasters preferred to hire people who spoke in this way. American accent was popularized by the famous news anchor <u>Walter Cronkite</u>.

People from Vernacular English have great difficulties understanding American English. In 21st century, as American companies spread worldwide, it became a survival need for other countries' corporate companies to hire the employees who can understand and talk to Americans.

Though, being an accent trainer, I would make this thing clear that the native English speakers from other countries like UK, Australia and Canada have no difficulties understanding American Accent. It is just an added flavor to them. It means <u>there is no much difference between American Accent and British Accent</u>. Truly speaking, in this book, I have emphasized on **INTERNATIONAL ENGLISH** which is a combination of both American and British Accent.

Let me make this point clear that learning pronunciation (which you have learnt from this book) does not mean you learn American English. You just learn Original English Pronunciation. And it is true that half of the world is still in darkness about understanding the pronunciation of Original International English. Some people, those who are negative to accepting new things, utter that learning pronunciation is of no use. But they never know what the market need. I am not saying that you learn pronunciation just to talk to Americans or British. What I am saying is that you learn pronunciation to talk to Americans or British or other native speakers for business requirement. Don't forget that you earn your living to survive, and the living is earned from market and in today's world – the market is based on communication – International Communication.

Learning English is not a matter of FUN, it is the need of your existence. The way the market is changing, expanding and being competitive day by day, it has come into the necessity of having the job-doers perfect with International Communication Skills. Now, communicating with the foreigners is not your entrainment but the basic requirement in commercial sectors. For the companies around the world, it is necessary to grow as well as expand, and just for that, they want human being equipped with communication talent.

Lesson 29
British English – American English
Here is a list of some words which are spoken differently in British and American English

British English	American English
Biscuit	Cookie
Lift	Elevator
Rubber	Eraser
Solicitor	Lawyer
Queue	Line
Post	Mail
Trousers	Pants
Hire	Rent
Holiday	Vacation
Advertisement	Commercial
Luggage	Baggage
Railway Station	Train Station
Autumn	Fall
Interval	Intermission
Sweets	Candy
Underground	Subway
Zed	Zee
Note	Bill
Booking	Reservation
Pavement	Sideway
Ground Floor	First Floor
Flyover	Overpass
Costly	Expensive
Tuition	Instruction
Reporter	News hawk

Oral reading

Jane and Peter's business relationship was deteriorating. There was a lack of communication between them and Jane was angry that Peter took no responsibility for this. She knew that Peter had not taken into account their economical situation when he decided to give their employees a salary raise. Peter, however, thought that he was aware of their annual budget and didn't see any reason to qualify his decision to Jane. Eventually, Jane contacted her stock broker in the USA in a futile attempt to cash in some of her shares. To her alarm, they were not worth enough to save the company, and Peter and Jane had to dissolve their partnership. Luckily, their friendship survived this ordeal and they still feel mutual respect for each other.

Lesson 30
English Slang

Slang is very informal way of speaking. It was considered below the level of standard educated speech. But now, as the density of the world is increasing fast, slag is being common. It consists of either new words or of current words employed in some new special sense. What is new and existing for one generation is old for the next. Old slang either drifts away or becomes accepted into the standard language, losing its eccentric color. Slang came in use from nineteenth century and has remained in use to the present day.

For example, the word 'flapper' is a slang which means a young woman who is unconventional and lively. And the word 'gay' for homosexual sense is slang, otherwise, the word 'gay' means cheerful.

This chapter is not to emphasize that you should be well-versed with slang, but just to make you familiar with it. Slang served many purposes being a private vocabulary binding people together. In the early years of nineteenth century, the term slang came to be applied much more generally to any language of a highly colloquial type consisting either of new words or of current words employed in some new special sense. Today, it is not wrong to say that not all colloquial or informal vocabulary is slang, but all slang is colloquial or informal.

Slang Word	Meaning
dogwatch	a night shift
gammon	insincere talk
jerk	a fool
loon	crazy
ort	buttocks
prob	problem
shypoo	inferior alcoholic drink
spic	Spanish language
stung	drunk
tart	girlfriend or wife
unstick	to take off

It may look strange to you but it is true that these are slang words and they are used in English. To get more words, you can buy Oxford Dictionary of Modern Slang or download it from internet.

Lesson 31
Figure of Expression

Language is the source of presenting expressions driven towards the sense. The meaning of a person's speech changes according to the way of his expression. In languages, the words are limited, but the senses are unlimited, and so, the human beings try to express their views going out of the words' boundary.

➢ <u>Imagery</u>
This is the way of creating images in the mind of the listeners. While speaking this way, the speaker creates an atmosphere so that the listeners should start imagining the things and they should feel it happening around them.
The moment I opened the door, I saw the smoke all around.
He tapped the head of lion and touched the tail of elephant.
➢ <u>Sarcasm</u>
This expression consists of bitter and wounding words as a result of annoyance delivered in a harsh tone.
The company's new policy is ripping off the customers. (Charging more money)
Now you are opening your big mouth. (Speaking too much)
➢ <u>Pleonasm</u>
Taking a round about and using more words than need in your speech is circumlocution. Generally this way of expression is used when you don't want to say something directly because it may hurt, so you make out an indirect way or you just want to make your speech more interesting.
I don't find it good to me. (It means I don't like it).
Of what good I am to you? (How may I help you?)
➢ <u>Idiomic</u>
Using idioms or phrases to mystify the speech is an idiomic expression.
Why are the politicians barking at the wrong tree? (Asking a wrong person or thing)
He paid the debt of nature. (He is dead)
➢ <u>Derogatory</u>
A remark of yours which is insulting or harmful to someone is a derogatory expression. People use it to show their anger or frustration in the speech.
The manager is a moronic personality. (Stupid)
The party high-command is playing a blind man's buff. (Unnecessary work)
➢ <u>Profanity</u> or <u>Coarse</u>
The use of an abusive language is profanity.
I gonna bang the son of b out.*
What made you ask him this f question?*
➢ <u>Rhetoric</u>
The language designed to persuade or impress some is rhetoric expression.
The inflation is bound to come.
The have to leave this city tonight.
➢ <u>Ellipsis</u>
An expression which is left half-spoken to the listener to figure out the obscurity of the meaning.
I don't know how I should find my ... but I need it very much.
The man behind this conspiracy was...you know who I am talking about.

Lesson 32
Figure of Speech
Figure of Speech is a departure from the ordinary form of expression, or the ordinary course of ideas in order to produce a greater effect.

<u>Metaphor</u>
The imaginative use of a word or phrase to describe something to show that the two have the same qualities:
He fought like a lion.
All the world's a stage and all the men and women merely players.

<u>Paradox</u>
The statement that contains two opposite ideas or seems to be impossible:
The child is the father of the man.
There was a stranger in the mirror.

<u>Hyperbole</u>
The speech using exaggeration by overstatement:
A hundred years should go to praise
Thine eyes and on thy forehead gaze

<u>Metonymy</u>
The fact of referring to something by the name of something else closely connected with it, used especially as a form of shorthand for something familiar or obvious:
I have been reading Shakespeare. (I have been reading the plays of Shakespeare)

<u>Personification</u>
The act of representing objects or qualities as human beings:
Love bade me welcome: yet my soul, guilty of dust and sin, drew me back.

<u>Apostrophe</u>
A direct address to the dead or to the absent:
O death! Where is your sting? O grave! Where is your victory?

<u>Euphemism</u>
A disagreeable thing by an agreeable name:
He has fallen asleep. (He is dead).

<u>Antithesis</u>
A striking opposition or contrast of words or sentiments in the same sentence to secure emphasis:
Man proposes, God disposes.

<u>Oxymoron</u>
The phrase that combines two words that seems to be the opposite of each other:
Parting is such sweet sorrow.
<u>Irony</u>
A mode of speech in which real meaning is exactly the opposite of that which is conveyed:
No doubt that you are the people and wisdom shall die with you. (You are fool).

Fallacy

Fallacy is the effect produced when animals and things are shown as having human feelings.
In John Milton's poem, Lycidas, the flowers are shown as weeping for the dead shepherd, Lycidas.

Onomatopoeia

The effect produced when the words used contain similar sounds to the noise they describe:
Murmuring of innumerable bees

Pun

The use of a word in such a way that it is capable of more than one application, the object being to produce a ludicrous effect:
Is life worth living? – It depends upon the <u>liver</u>.
An ambassador is an honest man who <u>lies</u> abroad for the good of his country.

Litotes

In Litotes an affirmative is conveyed by negation of the opposite, the effect being to suggest a strong expression by means of a weaker. It is opposite of Hyperbole.
I am a citizen of no mean (=a very celebrated) city.
The man is no fool (=very clever).
I am a little (=greatly) surprised.

Rhetorical Question

In this figure a question is asked not for the sake of getting an answer, but to put a point more effectively.
Am I my brother's servant?

Climax

The arrangement of a series of ideas in the order of increasing importance:
What an idea! Simple, severe, austere, sublime!

Archaism

The use of an old and obsolete word:
Don't you thou me.

Double negative

The construction that can be used as an expression and it is the repetition of negative words:
She doesn't know nothing about it.

Alliteration

The repetition of r sound:
A round the rugged rocks the rugged rascal ran.

Sibilance

The repetition of s sound:
Sister Suzy sewing socks for soldiers.

Adverbial Emphatic

It is used to stress on the meaning:
And next came her sister. | Little did I know about him.

Lesson 33
Homophones
This last lesson enlists some homophones of English. Find out the correct pronunciation of each word from your dictionary and practice over them.

personal
personnel
systemic
systemic

operation
oppression
bazaar
bizarre

vague
vogue
coarse
course

council
counsel
farther
father

flow
flaw
foreword
forward

martial
marital
formerly
formally

ordinance
ordnance
continually
continuously

Lesson 34
Relativity

This is the most unique lesson of this book. It explains the relativity of some Basic English words with three major foreign languages. Why it is necessary is that English itself is made of French and German, and for studying English Diction, we should know the sources of some words and their pronunciation. For each foreign language word the pronunciation is given in bracket.

English	French	Spanish	German
Mother	mère (meər)	madre (maadrey)	Mutter (mooteyr)
Father	père (peər)	padre (paadrey)	Vater (faateyr)
Brother	frère (freər)	hermano (hermaano)	Bruder (broodeyr)
Sister	soeur (soyer)	hermana (hermaanaa)	Schwester (shwesteyr)
Face	figure (figyuir)	rostro (rostro)	Gesicht (geyzisht)
Head	tête (teyt)	cabeza (kaabetha)	Kopf (kopəf)
Mouth	bouche (boosh)	boca (bokaa)	Mund (moont)
Apple	pomme (pom)	manzana (manthanaa)	Apfel (aafeyl)
Water	eau (au)	agua (aaguaa)	Wasser (vaaseyr)
Milk	lait (ley)	leche (lechey)	Milch (milsh)
Orange	orange (oraanzh)	naranja (naraankha)	Apfelsine (aafelziney)
One	une (iyuin)	una (unaa)	eins (aa-ins)
Two	deux (dyui)	dos (dos)	zwei (ts-vei)
Three	trois (troaa)	tres (tres)	drei (drei)
Monday	Lundi (lyuindi)	lunes (loones)	Montag (montaak)
Tuesday	Mardi (maardee)	martes (martes)	Dienstag (deenstaak)
Wednesday	Mercredi (merkredee)	miércoles (mi-er-koles)	Mittwoch (mitvokh)

Note: The 'ə' sign is valued 'half a' in pronunciation. The small 'n' is for nasal 'n' sound, and 'zh' is for 'zh' sound as in 'pleasure' word of English.

Lesson 35
Origin

As already said in the beginning, this book is for advanced learners of English accent, and so this lesson is going to explain you the most surprising things which are related to the origin of English. It enlists the alphabets of all the four languages with their pronunciation so that you can understand how much similarity is there among these four leading languages of the world.

English	French	Spanish	German
A	A (aa)	A (aa)	A (aa)
B	B (bey)	B (bey)	B (bey)
C	C (sey)	C (they)	C (tsey)
D	D (dey)	D (dey)	D (dey)
E	E (ey)	E (ey)	E (ey)
F	F (eff)	F (effey)	F (eff)
G	G (zhey)	G (hey)	G (gey)
H	H (aash)	H (aachey)	H (haa)
I	I (ee)	I (ee)	I (ee)
J	J (zhee)	J (hota)	J (ye)
K	K (kaa)	K (kaa)	K (kaa)
L	L (ell)	L (elley)	L (ell)
M	M (emm)	M (emmey)	M (emm)
N	N (enn)	N (enney)	N (enn)
O	O (o)	O (o)	O (o)
P	P (pey)	P (pey)	P (pey)
Q	Q (kyui)	Q (koo)	Q (koo)
R	R (err)	R (errey)	R (err)
S	S (ess)	S (essey)	S (ess)
T	T (tey)	T (tey)	T (tey)
U	U (eui)	U (oo)	U (oo)
V	V (vey)	V (vey)	V (fow)
W	W (dobl-vey)	W (dobl-vey)	W (way)
X	X (ikss)	X (eykis)	X (ikss)
Y	Y (eegreyk)	Y (ee-grey-gaa)	Y (ipselon)
Z	Z (zed)	Z (they-taa)	Z (tsaa-it)

Now you may have understood that most of the European languages have same alphabets, and their pronunciations are also similar. The purpose of this lesson is not to teach you French or Spanish here, but to make you aware of the source through which English created its own pronunciation. Remember that English has nothing of its own, and everything is taken from other languages. And the both simplicities and difficulties of English are the result of the adoption of the various things that took place in English.

Lesson 36
Base Matrix

Now we are going to see the linkage of English with Greek and Hebrew languages. Hebrew is the oldest language of the world which started with human civilization at Nile River in Mesopotamia. See the pronunciation of Hebrew letters and try to understand how they got transformed in Greek, Arabic, French, Spanish, German, and then English.

Greek Alphabets		Hebrew Alphabets	
A	alpha	א	alef
B	beta	ב	bet
Γ	gamma	ג	gimel
Δ	delta	ד	dalet
E	epsilon	ה	he
Z	zeta	ו	waw
H	eta	ז	zayin
Θ	theta	ח	het
I	iota	ט	tet
K	kappa	י	yod
Λ	lambda	כ	kaf
M	mu	ל	lamed
N	nu	מ	mem
Ξ	xi	נ	nun
O	omicron	ס	samekh
Π	pi	ע	ayin
P	rho	פ	pe
Σ	sigma	צ	tsade
T	tau	ק	qof
Y	upsilon	ר	resh
Φ	phi	ש	shin
X	chi	ת	taw
Ψ	psi		
Ω	omega		

The language science says that English is born to French and German, French and German are born to Latin and Greek, and Latin and Greek are developed from Hebrew. And before Hebrew there was no human language in the world. We should be thankful to English for its easy pronunciation; otherwise, the other old languages have very difficult pronunciation. Believe me, English is much easier than any other languages introduces in last two lessons.

Lesson 37
Commonly Mispronounced Words

In today's world, having working knowledge of English doesn't work. You should have proper knowledge of English. To rid of human life from difficulties we have to rise up the level of education. Try to learn correct pronunciation of words so that you should be able to understand others and they should also understand you.

cadre (**kaar**der)
marijuana (maariyu-**aa**naa)
bosom (**b**oozom)
vengeance (**v**endʒəns)
en route (aan root)

atheism (ə-**thee**-izm)
benign (bi**n**ain)
bestiality (beestiælty)
castle (**k**aasl)
chaos (**k**ei-os)

chauvinist (**sh**awvinist)
cuisine (kwi**z**een)
debauchee (di**b**awchi)
eunuch (**y**oonk)
facetious (faasee-ʃəs)

faux pas (faw paa)
fellatio (fəleiʃio)
idée fixe (eedei feex)
posthumous (pos-**t**yums)
panacea (pænaa-**see**-aa)

usurer (**y**oozərər)
xenophobe (zeno**f**ob)
vague (**v**eig)
avalanche (ə**v**elaansh)
envelope (envəlaup)
rendezvous (**r**ondevoo)

There are some more words whose correct pronunciation should be taught to English learners. What you can do is that you can make your own list of words and find out their pronunciation in dictionary. It will help you speak English correctly.

Lesson 38
Homophones

This lesson enlists some homophones of English. Find out the correct pronunciation of each word in your dictionary and practice over them.

lesson
lesion
melody
malady

systematic
systemic
power
prowess

faces
feces
balance
valance

vogue
vague
stair
satyr

rough
rouge
operation
oppression

possible
plausible
accusation
execution

fatality
futility
genres
generous

poverty
puberty
relevance
reverence

Lesson 39
Cluster Words

This lesson enlists the words of a group. Getting acquainted with correct meaning of these words will definitely take you miles ahead in learning English.

theism
atheism
monotheism
polytheism
all-theism
pantheism

sense
sensible
sensitive
sensor
sensual
sensuous

human
humane
humanism
humanitarian
humanize
humanoid

personal
personnel
persona
personage
personality
personification

literate
literacy
literary
literature
literati
literalism

Lesson 40
Evolution

This lesson explains the surprising thing that happened in English at the time of its birth. The words of English were created by altering many of the foreign words. Here is a list of some of them which clearly shows the evolution that took place in English.

The word **School**
It is an altered version of the combination of two words.
French: école (ekol)
German: Schule (shoolay)

The word **Marriage**
It is slightly changed in spelling but majorly in pronunciation from French.
French: mariage (maareezh)
Spanish: matrimonio (maatrimonio)

The word **Autumn**
It is a modified version of French word in the view of its Spanish equivalent.
French: automme (awton)
Spanish: otoño (otonio)

The word **Brown**
It is quite similar to its equivalent in German and French.
German: braun (braa-un)
French: brun (bru-ain)

The word **Uncle**
It is quite similar to its equivalent in French and German.
French: oncle (onkl)
German: Onkel (onkel)

The word **Animal**
It is quite similar to its Spanish and French equivalent.
Spanish: animal (aanimaal)
French: animal (aaneemaal)

The word **Tomato**
French: tomate (tomaat)
Spanish: tomato (tomato)
German: Tomate (tomaatey)

The evolution of English words is very interesting. What we learn today, took a lot of time to get well-placed in English. And so, we should thank the time for gifting us English as the most beautiful, easy, and pleasant language.

Lesson 41
Articulation
Articulation comes from the Latin word for "jointed" or "divided into joints." Articulation is the act of expressing something in a coherent verbal form, or an aspect of pronunciation involving the articulatory organs. This noun also describes the act of joining things in such a way that makes motion possible. Learn to pronounce these words following pronunciation hint given in brackets.

hyperbole (hai**pər**bəlee)
epitome (ə**pit**əmee)
montage (mon**taa**ʒ)
martyr (**maar**tər)
genre (**ʒaan**rər)
caveat (**kæ**viat)
debris (de**bree**)
façade (fə**saad**)
subtle (**sə**tl)
chignon (**ʃee**nyon)

bathe (beið)
entrepreneur (**on**trəprənyuər)
paradigm (**pe**rədyəm)
Greenwich (**gre**nitʃ)
panacea (panə**see**ə)
paramour (**pe**rəmuər)
species (**spee**ʃeez)
camouflage (**kæ**məflaaʒ)
visage (**vi**zidʒ)
prima facie (prima feishee)

chassis (**tʃ**æsee)
manoeuvre (mə**noo**vər)
furlough (**fə**rlou)
cucumber (**ky**ookəmbər)
tomb (toom)
apostle (ə**paw**səl)
avalanche (**æ**vəlænʃ)
almond (**aa**mənd)
masseur (mæ**sur**)
dough (dou)
convalesce (kawnvə**les**)
conscientious (kɒnʃee**en**ʃəs)
alumnus (ə**lə**mnəs)
poignant (**poi**nyənt)

Lesson 42
Hypercoinage

In this lesson you are going to learn the logic, reason or history of the formation of some well-known proper noun words.

Accenture	-	Accent on the future
Adidas	-	Acronym of the founder's name – Adi Dassler
Cisco	-	Shortened for San Francisco
Ferrari	-	The founder's name – Enzo Ferrari
Fiat	-	Fabbrica Italiana Automobili Torino
HMV	-	His Master's Voice
IBM	-	International Business Machine
Intel	-	Integrated Telecom
Toyota	-	The founder's name – Sakichi Toyoda
Vodafone	-	Acronym of Voice, Data and Telephone
Wipro	-	Western India Palm Refined Oil
Mozilla	-	One who kills Godzilla
Wikileaks	-	The lost leaks
MRF	-	Madras Rubber Factory
Wikipedia	-	Lost Encyclopedia
Adobe	-	The name of a river behind the founder's building
McDonald's	-	The surname of the founder
Levi's	-	The first name of the founder – Levi Strauss
Volkswagen	-	People's car (German language)
Chevrolet	-	The surname of the founder Louis Chevrolet
Java	-	The programmers' liking for the coffee of Java, Indonesia

Lesson 43

Symposium

As a leader, you must build lots of different skills to succeed, and one of these is public speaking. Several different elements contribute to the delivery of a powerful public speaker, and these are important for you to set yourself up for success. In this lesson, we'll provide you with some insight into the seven main elements of public speaking. Understanding these elements of public speaking is essential. Once you're familiar with the different components, you can organize and deliver your speech more effectively.

1. **Hyponym**
   The usage of words in more specific sense.
   Please **come** again. (come = say)
   His son is managing a big **empire**. (empire = business)
   She strongly believes in the **Supreme**. (Supreme = God)

2. **Circumlocution**
   A round-about expression.
   He wants you for his **life**. (life = marriage)
   Of what help I can be to you? (how may I help you)
   What brings you here? (What's your purpose)

3. **Eloquence**
   A convincing way of speaking mostly used by motivators.
   I have reasons to believe that…
   On the fair ground of humanity…
   It is something beyond nonsense…

4. **Lilting**
   Spoken or written in a metre of prosody.
   The rays of gaze are ablaze on her face.
   A kiss in life is the bliss of life.
   The dying euphoria is the diversion of his doctrine.

5. **Enigma**
   Extreme literary decoration and hypothesis.
   The thousands and thousands of beautiful faces I can see around.
   This is amazing and exhilarating moment for all of us.

6. **Granoquence**
   The usage of complex words.
   The public waiting for panacea fell into flamboyant subterfuge.
   The turbulence created by the anarchists caused turmoil all around.

7. **Colloquialism**
   Ordinary or familiar conversation.
   I **did** English in school. (did = learnt)
   How are the mangoes **going** these days? (going = selling)
   You need to **grow up** dude. (grow up = be wise)

Lesson 44
Paralogue
Paralogue is the study part of English pronunciation science. It defines how your statements or words are related the previous or ancient version of the language.

Old English
In 5th century, the German tribal of Anglia peninsula settled in the British island. They initially spoke four different dialects namely Saxon, Mercian, Northumbrian, and Kentish. The Saxon dialect, which was near to German language, developed into a language that we call Old English.

Saxon		English
aan	=	one
twa	=	two
threo	=	three
feowor	=	four
fif	=	five

Middle English
Middle English is the form of English spoken from the time of Norman (French) Conquest in British Islands from 1066 until 15th century. During these era of four hundred years, the Norman kings in Britain spoke their Norman language which was a variety of French language. When this Norman language of Britain (Anglo-Norman) merged with Old English (altered Saxon), it developed into a new language that we call Middle English.

Middle English		English
oon	=	one
two	=	two
three	=	three
fower	=	four
five	=	five

Modern English
English underwent extensive sound changes during the 15th century. While its spelling remained constant. Modern English was made of Great Vowel Shift. This language was further transformed by the spread of standardized London-based dialect in government and administration. As a result, starting from Geoffrey Chaucer (father of English literature) era, this language acquired self-conscious terms such as – Accent.

By the time of William Shakespeare, the language had become clearly recognizable as Modern English. In 1604, the first English dictionary was published – The Table Alphabeticall.

Lesson 45

Reservoir

Reservoir is a process when an imagined rule is applied to a context of a language with the belief of simplification. Though it begets unscientific or illogical results, but the cycle of time accepts those changes. It is the pronunciation of words, or word forms, which brings a language into major change. English did not have any authoritative body codifying (writing) norms of standard usage, unlike other languages, such as Arabic and French.

To reduce the increasing reputation of German and French in England, the hypercorrection wave started in the region. This wave targeted the German and French words which were newly adopted into English. As a result, the pronunciation (sometimes spelling) of these words were changed to defamiliarize them from their origin. This process gave birth to the culture of silent letters in English.

English	-	know
Old English	-	knowen
Old German	-	kneana

English	-	knife
Old English	-	cnif
Old German	-	knif

Another wave started in English when they started borrowing words of Greek and Latin. They removed the initial 'p' and 'b' sound of Greek and Latin words, and sometimes changed spelling, to make the pronunciation simple. The process was widely supported by the printing press coming to England. The printers belonged to German and France and they had German supported technology. But the printers, having free power, started adding something extra to the spelling of English words – just to make them acquainted to the way thy pronounced them in their own countries.

| English | - | psychology |
| Greek | - | psychology ('p' pronounced) |

| English | - | doubt |
| Latin | - | dubitare ('b' pronounced) |

Silent Letters Exercise

The rouge knight doubted that the asthmatic knave in knickers could climb the castle columns, but when their wrangle wrought chaos on the couple, the knight resigned with the knowledge that their tight-knit friendship wouldn't succumb to dub disputes.

Lesson 46
Good Voice Technique

An aspirant well trained on Voice Accent and Diction, can work as a newscaster, video jockey, radio jockey, movie artist, voice-over artist, singer, anchor, BPO executive, MNC executive, and orator. The following key points are helpful to Impressive Speaking Skill.

1. **Accurate Diction**
   Recognize your voice and try to make it better using connect pronunciation. Then concentrate on the accent part of the language and develop your ability to speak that way. You can record yourself reading poetry and parts of plays.

2. **Pause Focus**
   The power of speech is contained in the silence that you create as you move from point to point. There are four kinds of pauses you can use to empower your lingual presentation. They are – The Sense Pause, The Dramatic Pause, The Emphatic Pause, and The Sentence Completion Pause.

3. **Create Resonance**
   Our best, strongest, attractive and most natural voice comes from our diaphragm. You need to breathe to the deepest to strengthen your voice. To breathe correctly, simply inhale anal let your belly rise, then exhale and let your belly fall.

4. **Avoid Fillers**
   The 'Ahs' and 'Uhms' sound white speaking is not good. This can irritate the audience while listening to the speaker, if one tends to keep on adding these fillers over and over. You need to practice speaking a lot to get rid of these fillers.

5. **Creativity**
   Creativity in your speeches comes from your general Knowledge and your mood. You improve your knowledge from books, and your mood depends upon your wellbeing. Before your speech, eat and drink water lightly. This ensures that you are bright and alert when you start speaking.

6. **Sense of Humor**
   Having a good sense of humor, like Friendliness and Civility, is the great oilers of the wheels of social and professional interaction. Amusing people, and these who are ready to be amused by others, are pleasant to be around. While giving reasons and explanations, maintaining fun in your speeches keeps your audience bound with you.

Lesson 47

Contronyms

Contronyms is a surprising thing of a language. Like other language, English also has contronyms. It means "a word having two meanings that contradict one another." A contronym is also called an auto-antonym. It's a word which has contradictory (or reverse) meanings depending on the context. Mastering these words will help you play with your language in front of audience.

Desperate
1. Restless; 2. Despondent

Paragon
1. Excellent; 2. Competition

Sanction
1. Approval; 2. Penalty

Subtle
1. Nice; 2. Complex; 3. Clever

Rum
1. Fantastic; 2. Ugly; 3. Eccentric

Flurry
1. Excitement: 2. Bewilderment; 3. Stir

Weather
1. Climate; 2. Storm

Peer
1. Aristocrat; 2. An equal

Fast
1. Rapid; 2. Fixed

To enjoin
1. To instruct; 2. To prohibit.

To overlook
1. To inspect; 2. To fail to notice.

To Table
1. To discuss a topic at a meeting; 2. To postpone discussion of a topic

Lesson 48

Protonyms

Protonyms is the original entity after which another entity is named without the entities being related. Here is a list of some Protonyms. It helps you improve your understanding for English in terms of using correct words in contradictory situations.

Photo, Picture, Image

Photo: anything taken by a camera.
Picture: a drawing or painting artwork.
Image: a visual object modified by a computer.

Buy, Purchase, Procure

Buy: for general commodities.
Purchase: for big products.
Procure: obtaining goods or services for business.

Sickness, Illness, Disease

Sickness: general feeling of discomfort.
Illness: state of poor health.
Disease: Deviation from a biological norm.

Play, Drama, Cinema

Play: a theatrical performance.
Drama: a form of written literature.
Cinema: a recorded performance.

Offence, Crime, Atrocity

Offence: a wrongdoing that may or may not be punishable.
Crime: a punishable act.
Atrocity: most serious crime.

Crazy, Mad, Insane

Crazy: an eccentric person.
Mad: a mentally ill person.
Insane: one having mental disorder.

House, Home, Residence

House: a building where you stay.
Home: any location where you stay with family.
Residence: a place of temporary stay.

Lesson 49
Paradigm Shift
Paradigm Shift is the shifting of a language term from its origin to a different sense. This is a delightful lesson for those who love English.

1. **Hip hip hooray!**
   It is a Latin expression that means – Jerusalem is lost! The call was recorded in England in the beginning of the 19th century in connection with making a toast. In this sentence, the word 'hip' is a Latin acronym of "Hierosolyma Est Perdita". It means "Jerusalem is lost". This term gained notoriety in the German 'Hep hep riots' of 1819. This violence was orchestrated against Jews in Bavaria state of Germany. Saying 'Jerusalem is lost' was to disgrace Jews in Christian world.

2. **Pluck you!**
   Before the Battle of Agincourt in 1415, the French, anticipating victory over the English, proposed to cut off the middle finger of all captured English soldiers. Without the middle finger, it would be impossible to draw the English longbow; and therefore, they would be incapable of fighting in the future. Much to the bewilderment of the French, the English won a major upset and began mocking the French by waving their middle fingers at the defeated French, saying "Pluck you!"

3. **Mamma mia!**
   The earliest known use of this popular interjection Mamma mia is in the 1820s in the writing of poet Lord Byron. Mamma mia is a borrowing from Italian into English. Mamma = mother; mia = my. This interjection means: O my mother! (Oh my God!).

4. **INRI**
   Many Catholics choose to wear a cross as a symbol of their faith. It should also be noted that most crucifixes include the sign 'INRI' across the top. INRI is the Latin abbreviation for "Iesus Nazarenus, Rex Iudaeorum" which means - Jesus of Nazareth, King of Jews.

5. **I am go.**
   It appears to be an incorrect sentence, but it is grammatically correct. The word 'go' is an adjective too, which means progressive. So I am go = I am progressive.

6. **Mother**
   Let's look at the word 'mother' in five different languages. German: mutter; French: mère; Spanish: madre; Sanskrit: mata; Arabic: umu. You see that each word has 'm' letter, which means 'm' sound. Do you know why? It is because a baby can pronounce the first easy sound as – 'm'.

7. **No future tense in English**
   I will play.
   This originally means - I wish to play. Because 'will' means 'to wish'.

Lesson 50
Pacemover

Whatever type of music you're into, learning English with songs will help you improve your listening and speaking skills, vocabulary and pronunciation. And most importantly, it'll make learning English really enjoyable and fun. Listening to English songs while seeing lyrics help you understand native pronunciation without which you cannot become an international professional speaker. Though Cambridge IELTS audio 1, and audio 2 will you tremendously in improving English listening skill.

Five best songs to learn English
1. I'm Alive by Celine Dion
2. Heal the World by Michael Jackson
3. Rhythm divine by Enrique Iglesias
4. Waiting For Tonight by Jennifer Lopez
5. Desert Rose by Sting

Five best novels to learn English
1. The Godfather by Mario Puzo
2. Bloodline by Sidney Sheldon
3. Gone Girl by Gillian Flynn
4. The Blind Assassin by Margaret Atwood
5. The Da Vinci Code by Dan Brown

Five best movies to learn English
1. The Godfather
2. Independence Day
3. Inception
4. Pirates of the Caribbean
5. The Da Vinci Code

Lesson 51
Lyricology

Lyricology is the practice of listening to songs while seeing lyrics. As a non-native English speaker, you need to practice over some songs to learn pronunciation and understand the pace. While practicing, you need to read the lyrics in the same speed as the song moves on. Here is one of the best songs of the world for lyricology.

Song – We Didn't Start the Fire
By – Billy Joel

Cromosys Publication

English Voice Accent and Pronunciation

Niranjan Jha Showman

Niranjan Jha Showman
Trainer, Author, Physician, Entrepreneur, Filmmaker, Activist
Founder – Cromosys Corporation
Education and Technology Research Center
www.facebook.com/cromosys
+91-9561450045
Nallasopara (W), Mumbai

Communicate with People

Listen to Them Carefully

Engage in Conversation

Develop Your Style

Read As Much As Possible

Speak Confidently

NIRANJAN JHA SHOWMAN

Founder - Niranjan Jha Showman

Education and Technology Research Center

Patankar Park, Nallasopara (W), Mumbai. +91-9561450045

Education, Technology, Publication, Healthcare, Newsmedia, Realtor, Filmmaking

www.facebook.com/cromosys

Cromosys Publication
Teach
Yourself
German
NIRANJAN JHA SHOWMAN

Cromosys Publication
Teach
Yourself
French
NIRANJAN JHA SHOWMAN

Cromosys Publication
Teach
Yourself
Spanish
NIRANJAN JHA SHOWMAN

Cromosys Publication

English
Voice
Accent and
Pronunciation

NIRANJAN JHA SHOWMAN

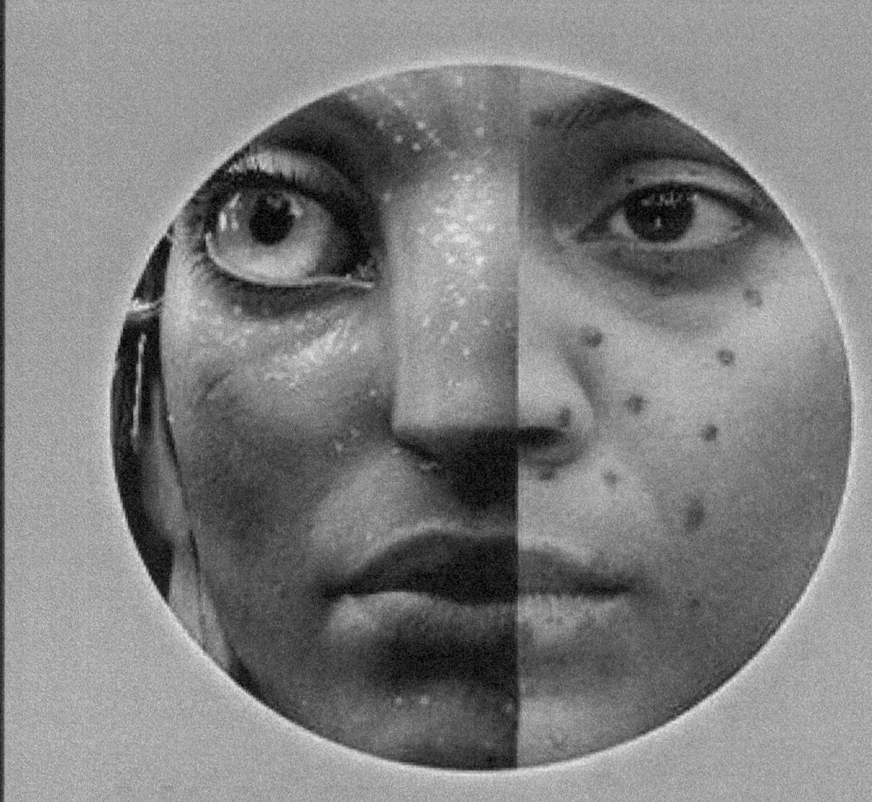

Teach
Yourself
Autodesk
MAYA
Cromosys Publication
NIRANJAN JHA SHOWMAN

Cromosys Publication
Teach
Yourself
Autodesk
3ds Max
NIRANJAN JHA SHOWMAN

Cromosys Publication
CRIMINAL FACTORY
NIRANJAN JHA SHOWMAN

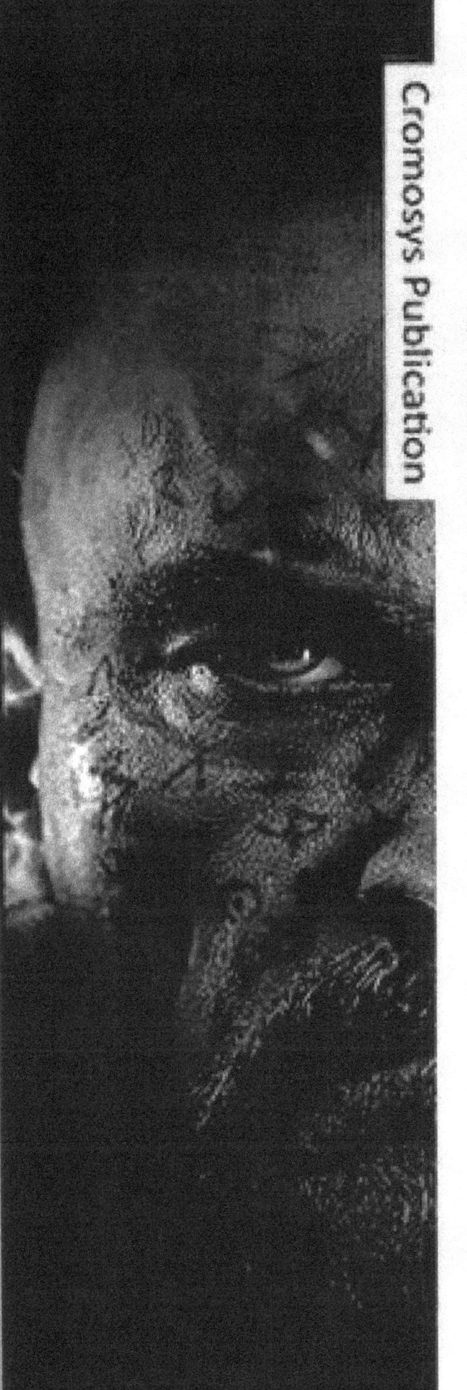

Cromosys Publication
FOCAL DISASTER
NIRANJAN JHA SHOWMAN

Cromosys Publication
Your talents will not help you succeed without your skill of using them.
NIRANJAN JHA SHOWMAN
BE
MILLIONAIRE
LIKE
ME

Extracts
from the Register
of Copyrights

Dated : 24/07/2020

1.	Registration Number	:	**L-76768/2020**
2.	Name, address and nationality of the applicant	:	NIRANJAN JHA SHOWMAN, CROMOSYS PUBLICATION, 001, JAYSATYAM, PATANKAR ROAD, NALLASOPARA (W), MUMBAI, MAHARASHTRA - 401203. INDIAN
3.	Nature of the applicant's interest in the copyright of the work	:	AUTHOR
4.	Class and description of the work	:	LITERARY / BOOK
5.	Title of the work	:	ENGLISH VOICE ACCENT AND PRONUNCIATION
6.	Language of the work	:	ENGLISH
7.	Name, address and nationality of the author and if the author is deceased, date of his decease	:	NIRANJAN JHA SHOWMAN, CROMOSYS PUBLICATION, 001, JAYSATYAM, PATANKAR ROAD, NALLASOPARA (W), MUMBAI, MAHARASHTRA - 401203. INDIAN
8.	Whether the work is published or unpublished	:	UNPUBLISHED
9.	Year and country of first publication and name, address and nationality of the publisher	:	N.A.
10.	Years and countries of subsequent publications, if any, and names, addresses and nationalities of the publishers	:	N.A. **SAME AS ABOVE**
11.	Names, addresses and nationalities of the owners of various rights comprising the copyright in the work and the extent of rights held by each, together with particulars of assignments and licences, if any	:	
12.	Names, addresses and nationalities of other persons, if any, authorised to assign or licence of rights comprising the copyright	:	N.A.
13.	If the work is an 'Artistic work', the location of the original work, including name, address and nationality of the person in possession of the work. (In the case of an architectural work, the year of completion of the work should also be shown).	:	N.A.
14.	If the work is an 'Artistic work', whether it is registered under the Designs Act 2000 if yes give details.	:	N.A.
15.	If the work is an 'Artistic work', capable of being registered as a design under the Designs Act 2000.whether it has been applied to an article though an industrial process and ,if yes ,the number of times it is reproduced.	:	N.A.
16.	Remarks, if any	:	

Diary Number :   7393/2019-CO/L
Date of Application :   09/05/2019
Date of Receipt :   09/05/2019

DEPUTY REGISTRAR OF COPYRIGHTS